ANGEROUSLY COOL PLACE...

D1508240

coke OR pepsi?

GIRL!

whaddya have
to say?

random thoughts
cool Q&A's
very ~~scientific~~
quizzes

coke OR pepsi?

G!RL!

CorP

Written and designed by
Mickey & Cheryl Gill

SCHOLASTIC INC.
New York Toronto London Auckland
Sydney Mexico City New Delhi Hong Kong

ISBN 978-0-545-28497-4

12 11 10 9 8 7 6 5 4 3 2 1   10 11 12 13 14 15/0

89

Printed in China

First Scholastic printing, September 2010

If you find this book
write A cool
Message here

If Bay found gross
this Keep

and send it
back to me. Thx,

Caera

owner's name here

1. Find out some pretty HILARIOUS stuff about your friends

2. Take a quiz that's anything but ordinary

3. Make a super cool accessory out of a page in the book

4. Give a shout-out to a friend

5. Save the world

And finally rip some pages out, write some random stuff, and hang it somewhere, anywhere. Oops, that's 6 reasons.

So get busy –
life as you know it
is about to change.

coke-or-pepsi.com

your initials C L H

Most people don't know that I

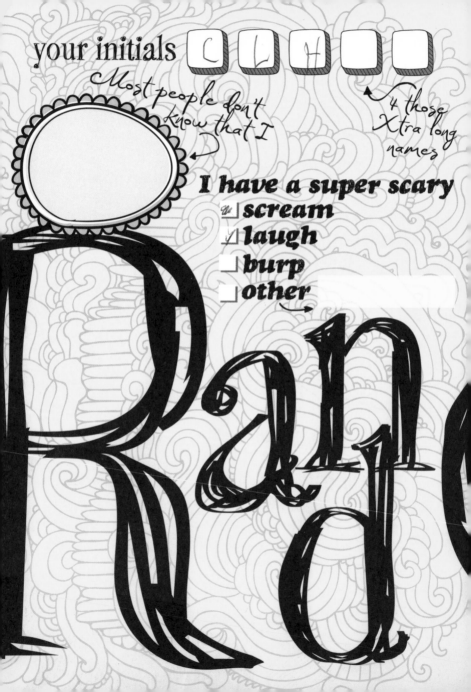

4 those Xtra long names

I have a super scary
- [x] scream
- [x] laugh
- [ ] burp
- [ ] other

Last person u lol with?

Trace your thumb or BIG TOE here. Finish drawing it.

I'm way better at

than most people.

Empty your backpack or bag. Look for something small. Tape it here.

1mo things about me & the world around me.

WHADDYA THINK OF WHEN U SEE THE WORD...

(IT CAN BE ANOTHER WORD, A SENTENCE,
A MEMORY,
OR EVEN AN ENTIRE STORY.)

HEART

BARK

GREEN

BUTTERFLY

CROWN

READ WORDS OUT LOUD AND WRITE DOWN THE ANSWERS.

HEART

BARK

GREEN

BUTTERFLY

CROWN

GRAB YOUR BEST FRIEND & TURN THIS UPSIDE DOWN.

OK,
WHAT DOES YOUR
BEST FRIEND
THINK OF WHEN
SHE HEARS
THE SAME WORDS?

The very scientific test for LOVE

Color a petal red each time your crush makes eye contact, smiles at, or says something nice about you (or says something wonderful about you to someone else).

Color a petal black for each time he has a chance but doesn't make eye contact, smile, or talk to you. Ugh!

Love Study Results from Noted Experts

lots of red petals

He definitely loves you and you'll probably get married, have five kids, and live in a big house someday.

half red petals, half black petals

Hmmm. He probably doesn't LOVE you, but let's not rule out LIKE just yet.

lots of black petals

It's most likely 1 of these 3.

a. He's just not that into you. His loss!

b. You're way cooler than he is, and he knows it.

c. He's noticed that you're always staring at him and scribbling in this book. And it's really freakin' him out!

IF YOUR FRIEND IS HAVING A SUPER BAD DAY

this book could really help.

**Cut out the mask to the right. Cut out eye holes.
Thread strings thru holes and tie it around your face.
(Wearing all black with tights too would be a nice touch.)**

Go see your friend. Tell her

I'm **Super Pits!** A.K.A. - Miss Cherry Maraschino, and I've come to save the day!

Yeah, it's stupid. Bet your friend will laugh though.

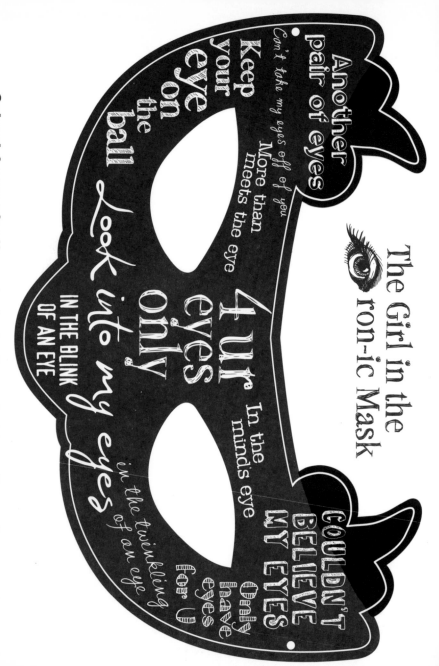

The Girl in the ron-ic Mask

Another pair of eyes

Can't take my eyes off of you

Keep your eye on the ball

More than meets the eye

Look into my eyes

4 ur eyes only

IN THE BLINK OF AN EYE

In the minds eye

in the twinkling of an eye

COULDN'T BELIEVE MY EYES

Only have eyes for U

MY LIFE IS SCRAP

Look for scraps of stuff from your daily life
(gum wrappers, fruit labels, notes, and on & on).
Tape them to this page. Write down where they came from.

DOT ALL OF THE i's WITH

ı   **I**   1   1

1   *l*   1   1

1   ı   1   *l*

i'm watching you

If you're right-handed, draw your best friend with your left hand. If you're a lefty, draw your bf with your right.

Draw a picture of yourself without using your hands. Hold a black marker between your teeth or toes.

She's soooo boring.

Dress her in your favorite outfit.

READ MY LIPS

1. Apply lipstick or lipgloss to lips.
2. Blot below.
3. Write name of kissable color next to it.
4. Repeat with other colors.

Now you have a lipstick log

Leave this page blank

IF YOU'RE FEELING SUPER SAD

THIS BOOK COULD REALLY HELP YOU.

Tear out this page

Crumble it up over and over again

Roll it between your hands until it's really soft

Wipe away your tears

Write the first letter of your first name here

. . . . .

Fill in the blanks with words or phrases that begin with this letter.

1. something you like to do _____

2. one of your favorite foods _____

3. excuse 4 not doing homework _____

4. animal _____

5. something in ur room _____

6. item of clothing _____

7. word u say a lot _____

8. person's last name _____

9. something sweet _____

10. something salty _____

ok, write your last name here

Circle the FIRST letter in your last name. Fill in the blanks with words or phrases that begin with the circled letter.

1. something a dog would eat _____

2. name of a place _____

3. reason to go to the doctor _____

4. name of an imaginary planet _____
   (that's right, make it up)

5. activity _____

6. reason for being late _____

7. something u liked when u were little _____

8. brand name _____
   (like Coke, Abercrombie, etc.)

9. something in a backpack _____

10. makeup product _____

DO NOT WRITE ON THIS PAGE. YOU'LL SEE WHY LATER.

WRITE SOMETHING
HERE IN THE
SECRET VAULT.
SOON, YOU'LL LOCK IT UP.

wish one

wish two

Make a wish on a shooting star. Write it on the tail. Poke holes in all the little circles.

Then glue or tape this page to the page behind it.

wish
three

wish four

wish
five

Glue or
tape this page
to the page
behind it.

DRAW SOME-
THING BEHIND
THE SECRET
DOOR. YOU'LL
BE CLOSING
IT SOON.

→TURN THAT PAGE OVER TO SEE WHY YOU DON'T WANT TO WRITE ON THIS PAGE!

COKE or PEPSI?

Ask yourself. Ask your friends.

draw it

1. What's your 1st memory? _____

2. ◯ Nutritious fruit smoothie   ◯ Decadent chocolate milkshake

3. CONFESSION TIME

Something u said u like because everyone else did (but secretly

you didn't)? _____ ◯ Huh?

4. What cool class do u wish your school offered? _____

5. I would never give up
   ◯ my cell phone
   ◯ the Internet
   ◯ toilet paper!

6. Something you do that bugs other
   people but you still do it? _____

   _____

7. Finish this sentence. I Love _____.

8. ◯ kill   ◯ Run from   ◯ Trap & release roaches. Ick!

9. What other language would u like 2 speak? _____

10. Had onion breath? ◯ Yes ◯ No How 'bout garlic? ◯ Yes ◯ No

OKE OR PEPSI?

Ask yourself. Ask your friends.

1. If you were a crayon, what color would you be? _____

2. Like to have your hair brushed? ○ Yes, feels great! ○ No way

3. Person you've talked to the most today? _____

4. Sitting on a seat that's been warmed by someone else?
○ Creepy ○ Fine, no prob

5. Favorite room color and Y? _____

6. Yummier smell?
○ Movie theater popcorn ○ Chocolate in a candy store

7. How do you feel about raisins? ○ Love 'em ○ Hate 'em Y?

8. Pets sleep in bed with you?
○ Yep, I snuggle with them ○ No ○ No pets

9. I ALWAYS forget _____.

10. What's on your bedroom floor? _____

_____

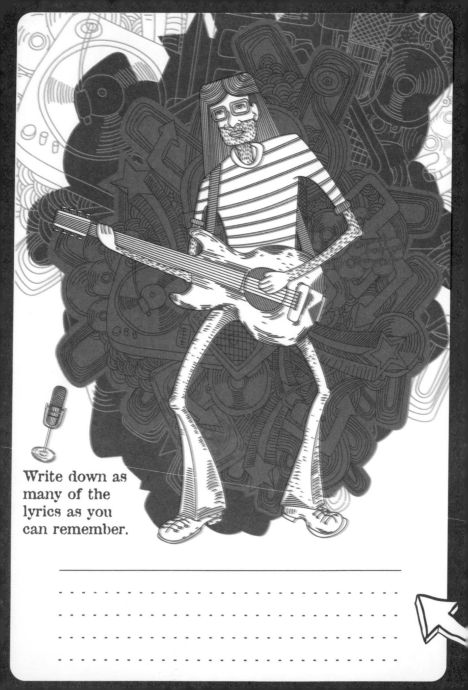

Write down as
many of the
lyrics as you
can remember.

COKE OR PEPSI?

Ask yourself. Ask your friends.

1. Last celebrity you read about? _____

2. Mixed vegetables ○ should be banned ○ are tasty!

3. Something you've tried & will never try/do again?

_____

4. Ever run a lemonade stand? ○ Nope ○ Yep

5. I'm in love with _____.

6. What's in your perfect taco? _____

7. Who makes u laff the hardest? _____

8. What weird food combo do you love? _____

_____

9. Ever been on crutches? ○ No ○ Yes. What 4? _____

_____

10. What's your absolute most favorite song right now?

Start your own
Paper Chain
letter

Emily   My cat   Brittany   Soccer   Chocolat

1. Write your name & something you love on a link.

2. Ask friends to do the same.

3. Cut out the links and tape together, like a chain.

4. Hang the paper chain and sign. (Turn 2 pages to find sign.)

5. Ask more friends to add links.

Check out paper chain letter at coke-or-pepsi.com

This is a
Paper Clip letter U

Name _____

loves _____

person, place, thing, activity

Name _____

loves _____

person, place, thing, activity

Name _____

loves _____

person, place, thing, activity

Name _____

loves _____

person, place, thing, activity

Name _____

loves _____

person, place, thing, activity

Name _____

loves _____

person, place, thing, activity

don't break the chain.

Name _____ **loves** _____
person, place, thing, activity

Name _____ **loves** _____
person, place, thing, activity

Name _____ **loves** _____
person, place, thing, activity

Name _____ **loves** _____
person, place, thing, activity

Name _____ **loves** _____
person, place, thing, activity

Hang this sign next to your paper chain

THIS IS A
PAPER CHAIN
LETTER. WRITE YOUR NAME
& SOMETHING YOU ♡ ON A
or someone
LITTLE PIECE OF PAPER
& ADD IT TO THE CHAIN.
*Don't
break
the
chain.*

WRITE A RAP
ABOUT SOMETHING DRAMATIC (OR NOT) THAT HAPPENED TODAY.

I'm
Just
SA

Let your friends say whatever they want in chalk.

'IN'

Erase. Start all over again.

WHICH IS THE WORST?

Rank them from 1-10.

10 being the most humiliating EVER!

Ask around. Did any of these ever happen to anyone you know?

☐ Made your big solo debut in front of entire school and forgot the lyrics to your song.

☐ Got a little too excited at a school pep rally and split your pants. Rip!

☐ Walked into the boys bathroom by mistake (and it's NOT empty). *Wrong do*

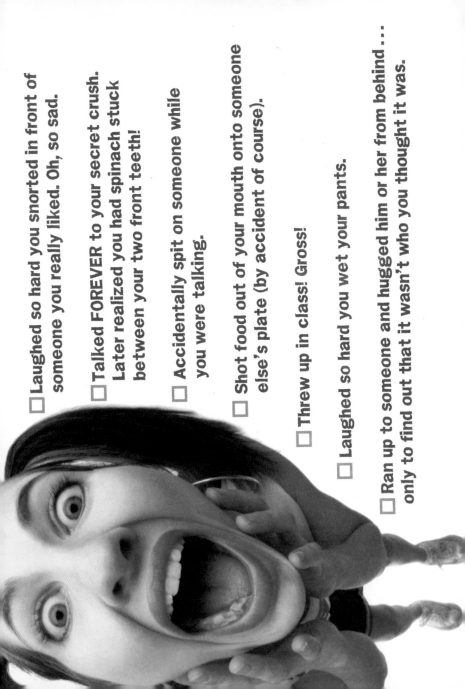

☐ Laughed so hard you snorted in front of someone you really liked. Oh, so sad.

☐ Talked FOREVER to your secret crush. Later realized you had spinach stuck between your two front teeth!

☐ Accidentally spit on someone while you were talking.

☐ Shot food out of your mouth onto someone else's plate (by accident of course).

☐ Threw up in class! Gross!

☐ Laughed so hard you wet your pants.

☐ Ran up to someone and hugged him or her from behind … only to find out that it wasn't who you thought it was.

Put this book under your

Write down a dream
the next morning.
(Keep this book
under your pillow
until you remember
a dream.)

Wear this Book

Make a cut paper cuff bracelet

1. Cut out a silver or gold cuff.

2. Cut out wings or jewels.

3. Wrap cuff around wrist, tape together, and cut off any extra cuff.

Fold tab down.   Fold tab under and glue to cuff.

Fold tab under along dotted lines & tape down to cuff.

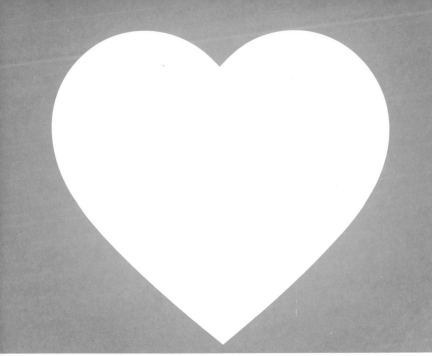

The itsy-bitsy Luv ya note.

1. Write a note in the above.

2. Cut it out.

3. Fold each side in like this. ⟶

4. Then fold top down.

5. Fold the flap up and seal with a sticker.

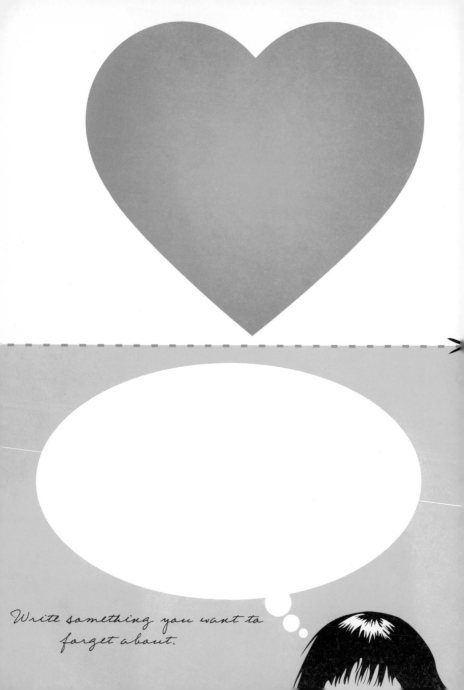

Write something you want to
forget about.

Have you ever
stuck a piece of gum
under a desk?

If yes, that's gross.

Well, here's your chance to do it
if you never have or if you need to
get it out of your system 1 last time.

1. Chew some gum.

2. Stick it here ———→
              under desk.

3. Cut left page in half,
   following the dotted line.

4. Fold over and stick to gum.

WHO WO[TO

Choose wisely (that super smart brainiac from school might be better than the cute kid at the smoothie place)

☞ ... were caught in the path of an oncoming twister ❓

☞ ... needed a partner for a popular TV dance show ❓

✦ ... had 1 day to convince aliens not take over the world ❓

D YOU CHOOSE
E WITH YOU IF
YOU...

Ask yourself.

k your friends.

my best friend

my brother

my fave movie star

hottie down the street

☞ **Why?** _____

_____

_____

☞ **Why?** _____

_____

_____

_____

☞ **Why?** _____

_____

_____

_____

For your pouty pucker, do you prefer…

- ○ #1 chapstick
- ○ 2b or not 2b. luscious lipstick
- ○ c. pink lipgloss
- ○ Triple D. all of the above

What feels most like you?

- ○ #1 t-shirt and jeans
- ○ 2b or not 2b. mismatched pieces I put together
- ○ c. trendy skirt & top
- ○ Triple D. all of the above

To satisfy the hungry girl within what sounds best?

- ○ #1 burger & fries
- ○ 2b or not 2b. Moo Shu pork
- ○ c. chicken & veggies
- ○ Triple D. all of the above

A cool Saturday would be

- ○ #1 movie with a few friends
- ○ 2b or not 2b. hang out with best friend
- ○ c. mall with a group of friends
- ○ Triple D. all of the above

Worst nightmare?

- ○ #1 friendship drama
- ○ 2b or not 2b. being told I'm average
- ○ c. nothing to wear
- ○ Triple D. all of the above

CHECK OUT
WWW.COKE-OR-PEPSI.COM
FOR EXTREMELY UNSCIENTIFIC,
NEVER TESTED BEFORE RESULTS.

coke
OR
pepsi?

Paint each toenail with different nail polish colors you like.

Check out your shoes. Write

Write the color name on each toe.

l the different brand names here.

If you need a good little laugh
(you know, not the tear-inducing, wet your pants, I can't breathe laughter), try this

{ Close your eyes and move a finger up and down this list and stop. Open your eyes and write the word you landed on in the space below. }

{ Now, do the same thing with this list of words. }

A

juicy
green
slippery
captain
sticky
lady

B

hairball
spittle bug
dumplings
gym socks
dung beetle
turkey legs

_____
Word from list A

_____
Word from list B

Write this word combo on different surfaces this week. Just cuz.

annals of the "Not~so~ Secret" Secret Society

What's the
Scariest
thing that's ever happened
to you?

Ask your friends. Ask yourself. Write the stories down.

I heard footsteps behind me.

I walked into class and didn't know there was a test.

I borrowed my sister's shirt without asking her and she...

I swear I saw a shadow following me....

turn

Take a vote
with all your friends.
Who has the scariest story ever?

N-S-S

Secret Society

Name

the brave
survived the most bone-chillin' event ever!

Now, ask each friend to give
you an awesome
"I'M SCARED TO DEATH"
scream.
(Don't do it in public.)
Vote on the Best.

The
N-S-S
Secret Society
Awards

Name

the title of the best
delivery of a
blood-curdling,
horror movie-
worthy
Scream!

What's the most Embarrassing thing that's ever happened to you?

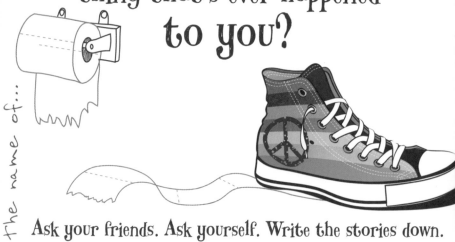

Ask your friends. Ask yourself. Write the stories down.

I couldn't remember the name of...

_____
_____
_____
_____
_____
_____
_____

I slipped on some ice cream at the mall and landed on my butt!

I went to school with a price tag hanging from my shirt...

turn →

If I spit on the guy who sits next to me...

Is this a word? ✓

Who has the Embarrassing-est story ever?

N-S-s

Secret Society

Name

is officially
Miss Mortified!

Do You Risk the Embarrassment?

What would u or your friends be willing to do on a dare?

wear a shirt inside out for a whole day?

fill in space between eyebrows with a brow pencil, creating a unibrow?

tape toilet tissue to the bottom of your shoe and drag it around the mall?

wear a homemade "women's restroom" sign on your back to a football game?

call someone by the wrong name repeatedly?

What's the
Worst Pain
you've ever felt?

Ask your friends. Ask yourself. Write the stories down.

allergic and it crushed me.   I tripped

I had to give my kitty away to a friend because I was

and busted my head open on a doorknob.

turn →

I accidentally squirted lemon into a gash...

Who has the most excruciatingly Painful story?

N-S-S
Secret Society

Adrianna
Name

is the Queen
of Pain!

How many of these have you (or friends) felt the Pain of?

- ✓ bee sting
- ○ wasp sting
- ○ jellyfish sting
- ○ ant bite
- ○ mosquito bite
- ○ spider bite
- ○ shark bite
- ○ dog bite
- ○ cat bite
- ○ vampire bite
- ○ snake bite
- ✓ little kid bite
- ○ cat scratch
- ○ sunburn
- ○ busted lip
- ○ broken arm
- ○ broken nose

- ○ broken leg
- ○ broken finger
- ○ broken toe
- ○ broken heart
- ○ bump on the head
- ○ iron burn
- ○ stove burn
- ○ paper cut
- ○ gaping wound
- ○ stitches
- ○ spanking! Yow!
- ○ splinter
- ○ pink eye!
- ○ earache
- ○ toothache
- ○ sore throat
- ○ needle shot

YUCK!

You have
a pair of Rollerblades, a bowl of spaghetti & meatballs and a rake.

What could you and a friend do with this stuff?
Ask around. Write your answers down.

_____

_____

_____

_____

_____

_____

you
must
think
outside
the
box

Have trouble writing papers for school?

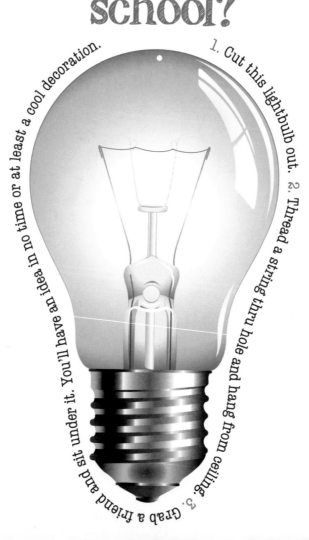

1. Cut this lightbulb out. 2. Thread a string thru hole and hang from ceiling. 3. Grab a friend and sit under it. You'll have an idea in no time or at least a cool decoration.

What's the most awesome pet (or wild animal) story, trick, whatever that you've heard.

Write the stories here.

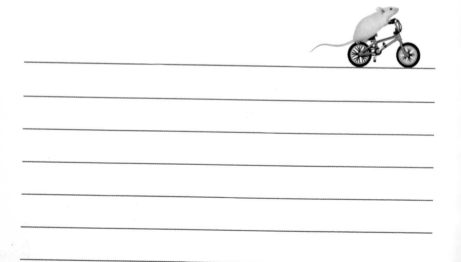

_____

_____

_____

_____

_____

_____

_____

Ask friends what's the funniest pet name they've ever heard. List them here.

Circle the most laff out loud one!

the

_____ _____
name   kind of animal or breed

the

_____ _____
name   kind of animal or breed

the

_____ _____
name   kind of animal or breed

the

_____ _____
name   kind of animal or breed

the

_____ _____
name   kind of animal or breed

the

_____ _____
name   kind of animal or breed

the

_____ _____
name   kind of animal or breed

the

_____ _____
name   kind of animal or breed

the

_____ _____
name   kind of animal or breed

the

_____ _____
name   kind of animal or breed

THIS IS A QUIZ.

IT'S OPEN BOOK. ASK YOUR FRIENDS FOR HELP. THERE'S NO TIME LIMIT.

1. Write down everything you like to EAT.

2. Write down anything you HATE to do.

3. Write down everything you LOVE (people, pets, sports, etc.)

Circle your ABSOLUTE FAVE! *Write it here.*	Circle the WORST! *Write it here.*	Circle 1 of your LOVES. *Write it here.*

You're a(n) —————— eating, —————— hating, —————— loving person.

SPRAY WHAT'S

Use paint, lipstick,
nail polish, whatever...
write what you've been dying to say.

Stuck in a boring situation?

Give LIFE to these
Inkblots

Add eyes, nose, ears, hats, boots, you name it.
Give them a car, scooter, or plane so they can escape this page.

Dear _____,

YOUR NAME

Love, your awesome self;

_____

YOUR NAME

Write a note to your future self. Fold note along dotted line and tape shut.

note to future self

DRAW YOUR BEST DOODLES
IN THIS SPACE.

WRITE DOWN HILARIOUS 😃 STORIES, LATEST CRUSH NEWS, WHATEVER U WANT. 👉 TAPE PICS, TICKETS, & NOTES DOWN TOO.

You think you're better than me?

STICK THIS→

STUFF UP

IN YOUR

LOCKER,

BEDROOM,

OR

WHEREVER

Go to
coke-or-pepsi.com
to download more copies.

Cut out and tape to your bedroom door.

Sun-Fri
24 HOURS
6 DAYS A WEEK
Sat
ALL HOURS
EXCEPT 3-3:15 AM

RESTROOM

Sat
3 AM - 3:15 AM

Cut out and tape to your bathroom door.

VISITORS

PLEASE REGISTER AT SECURITY OFFICE

Cut out and tape to your bedroom door.

ONE
WAY

MINE →

Cut out and tape wherever you want. You are the boss.

NO
CUTE SHIRT,
CUTE SHOES,
N⊘
ENTRY

Cut out and tape to your bedroom door. Keep out.

Please Take a Number

1 2 3 4 5 6 7

Cut out sign. Cut along dotted lines. Tape anywhere you want.

Tear out this page.

Cut out pocket and
tape or glue to inside
back cover of book.

This is where I stopped.

Tear out this page.

Cut
bookmark
out
and
fold
along
dotted
line.

GIRL! Creators

Mickey
Something unusual about u?
Grew up on a catfish farm.
Coke or Pepsi? Coke, always.
Collect anything? Converses.

. Cheryl
Something you like that most
people don't? TV ads.
Collect anything? Scarves and
little soap figurines. Weird.
Whaddya love? Asking people
lots of questions.

Hawkeye (our muse)
Fave thing to do?
Sneak out of the house.
Coke or Pepsi? Huh?
What scares you? Plastic bags.